OUR LIFE TOGETHER:
A COUPLE'S JOURNAL

A COUPLE'S JOURNAL

Our Life Together

A MEMORY BOOK
TO CAPTURE OUR LOVE

SHANE KOHLER

ROCKRIDGE
PRESS

First Rockridge Press hardcover edition 2022

Rockridge Press and the Rockridge Press logo are trademarks or registered trademarks of Callisto Media Inc. and/or its affiliates in the United States and other countries and may not be used without written permission.

For general information on our other products and services, please contact our Customer Care Department within the United States at (866) 744-2665, or outside the United States at (510) 253-0500.

Hardcover ISBN: 978-1-68539-920-7
Paperback ISBN: 978-1-68539-269-7

Manufactured in the United States of America

Interior and Cover Designer: Amanda Kirk
Art Producer: Hannah Dickerson
Editor: Kahlil Thomas
Production Editor: Dylan Julian
Production Manager: David Zapanta

Illustrations © Julia Dreams/Creative Market and Minkina/Creative Market. Letterpress © artimasa/Creative Market.

10 9 8 7 6 5 4 3 2 1 0

These memories belong to:

_____

and

_____

Contents

Welcome to Your Memory Book

Contained within these pages are special opportunities to document, commemorate, and remember the special moments of your life together and the love you share with each other. As you go through each page of this book together, you will reflect on the key moments of the past that brought you to where you are today. You will experience gratitude and thankfulness for what you share right now in the present. And you will imagine and dream up your future together.

This book is for all couples. Whether you've been together only a short time or you're commemorating a lifetime of love, this book will give you the opportunity to acknowledge your love and appreciate yourself and your partner for everything you've both brought to this partnership.

Each part of this book will allow you to view your relationship from a different perspective. Beginning with "How We Met" and ending with "Picturing Our Future Together," you'll explore your adventures, celebrations, significant relationships, and everything in between! Each part will include insightful prompts and activities that guide you into deeper connection and appreciation. All you have to do is let yourselves go and follow the prompts to create hours of sharing, laughter, and intimacy. When you're finished, you'll have a book of memories that will last a lifetime.

There's no right way to go through this book. You can begin anywhere you want, go through the parts in any order you want, and answer the prompts in whatever way feels authentic for you. There's also no deadline to complete this. The only purpose is to experience the joy and connection of being in love and to document the important moments in your relationship so you have them for years to come.

In the beginning of this book, you'll find a page titled "A Picture of Us" where you can attach a favorite photo of you both. Following that, you'll find a page titled "A Letter to Us" where you and your partner can set intentions for how you want to navigate the book together and anything you want to share before beginning. The end of each part will contain a two-page spread for mementos that correspond to that part's theme. Feel free to use this space to write, draw, or attach anything you want. In the back of the book, you'll find a page for each of you titled "My Letter to You" where you will each write a letter to your partner reflecting on your experience completing the book together and share your thoughts and feelings with each other.

Take this opportunity to express your love in a unique way, open and pour out your hearts to each other, appreciate the love that you share, and document the pivotal moments you never want to forget. Many blessings on this journey for you both! May your hearts be full; may you feel safe, loved, and protected; and may you complete this book with a new appreciation for your life and love together.

A PICTURE OF US

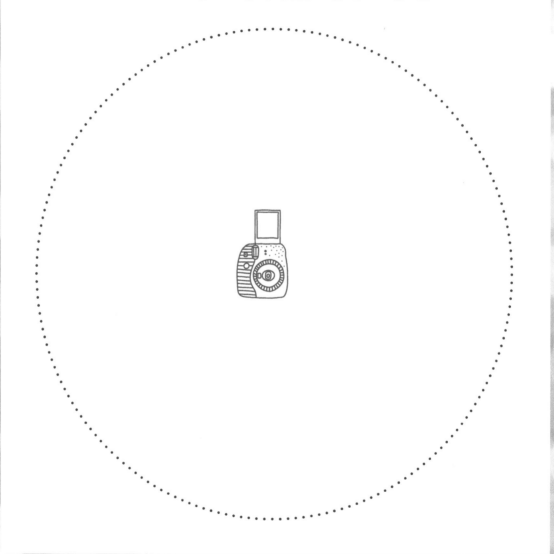

A LETTER TO US:
How We Will Reflect on Our Life Together

_____

_____

_____

_____

_____

_____

_____

_____

_____

PART 1

How we met

This is the beginning of our story, where it all began.
These are the magical moments that shaped the magic
we call our life today. We are not the people we were
back then, but we couldn't be us if not for them. As we
reflect on who we were and where we came from, we find
immense appreciation for who we are and where we are
today, for the love and life we share, and for the beauty
that is all around us.

Until You Came into My Life

It's so interesting to consider how it all happened for us.
Many things had to align for us to be here now.
So much has changed since then, and we've changed so much!

Let's take a moment and remember who we were
and where we were in our lives at that time.

_____	_____
_____	_____
_____	_____

When I met you, I was _____ years old.

When I met you, I was _____ years old.

I was living at _____ (location)

I was living at _____ (location)

with _____ (roommates/pets)

with _____ (roommates/pets)

I spent a lot of time with/doing

I spent a lot of time with/doing

For work, I

For work, I

I would often _____ for fun.

I would often _____ for fun.

About That Time

During that time in our lives, I remember . . .

_____   _____
_____   _____
_____   _____
_____   _____
_____   _____
_____   _____
_____   _____
_____   _____
_____   _____
_____   _____
_____   _____
_____   _____
_____   _____
_____   _____

Our First Meeting

As we think back on that time, it's beautiful to consider how innocent we were, how little we knew about what would happen, how our hopefu hearts had found something so special and didn't even know it yet.

Looking back on that day, my initial thoughts are . . .

The Where and When

We first met at

_____
(location)

_____

It was

_____
(time of year)

_____

in _____
(city/country/state)

I was there because . . .

_____   _____

_____   _____

_____   _____

_____   _____

When I first met you, my thoughts were . . .

_____   _____

_____   _____

_____   _____

_____   _____

The thing I'll never forget about that day is . . .

_____   _____

_____   _____

_____   _____

_____   _____

Let's Be Artists

Draw a sketch that symbolizes something about our first meeting and see if we can guess the meaning of each other's drawings.

No Accidents

Call it fate, chance, or happenstance. Many things could have prevented us from being together, but they didn't affect us. We were right where we were supposed to be, at the exact right time, so we could find each other and create the love we share today. Let's reflect on how it all came together.

Our first meeting was . . .
☐ Planned | ☐ A chance encounter

We met through/because of . . .

_____   _____

I was living in_____   I was living in _____
                    (city)   *(city)*

at that time because _____   at that time because _____

_____   _____

I almost didn't _____,   I almost didn't _____,

_____   _____

_____ but I'm glad I did.   _____

                                        _____ but I'm glad I did.

When I think of how we met, I . . .

_____   _____

_____   _____

At First Sight

The first time we saw each other, time stood still.

When I first saw you, you were

_____
(standing/sitting)

in _____
(location)

doing _____

When I first saw you, you were

_____
(standing/sitting)

in _____
(location)

doing _____

When I saw you, I thought to myself . . .

_____

_____

_____

_____

When I think of our first meeting, the feeling I have is . . .

_____

_____

_____

_____

_____

_____

I knew this was something special when . . .

_____

_____

_____

_____

I Don't Want to Miss a Thing

Let's paint the picture clearly to commemorate
that special moment for all time, leaving nothing out.

Our first meeting was . . . ☐ Indoors | ☐ Outdoors

What I remember most about the place we met is . . .

_____   _____

I was wearing . . .

_____   _____

The weather that day was . . .

_____

We spent _____ together that day.
(amount of time)

I left feeling . . .

_____   _____

_____   _____

Other details I remember are . . .

_____   _____

_____   _____

Only Seconds and Inches

It's easy to take for granted how it all happened, but the truth is that our destinies lie only in seconds and inches. If certain things had happened—which could have happened easily—we might never have met at all!

Let's play a game. Think of how many things could have prevented our meeting, and as we see these in front of us, it will help us appreciate how blessed we truly are.

Those Who Were There

There is usually someone (or a few people) who play a big part in two people coming together. Maybe it was a friend or confidant who talked us through our fears, the person who introduced us to each other or the people who cheered us on along the way.

As we think of the others who had an important role in our love, who are the people that stand out the most?

_____   _____

_____   _____

_____   _____

Are these people a part of our life today?

_____   _____

_____   _____

In what way do they play a role in our life?
If we've lost touch, do we want to rekindle the relationship?

_____   _____

_____   _____

_____   _____

_____   _____

What Makes Us Special

Every love story has something special about how it began. There's something that is unique only to our love, something that sets our story apart from all others.

What is uniquely special about how we met?

_____   _____

_____   _____

_____   _____

_____   _____

Can you think of something from the day we met that I don't know yet?
Maybe it was a stolen moment or a special surprise you tried to plan.

_____   _____

_____   _____

_____   _____

_____   _____

What's your favorite thing about how we met?

_____   _____

_____   _____

_____   _____

_____   _____

Gratitude

When I think of the day we met, I am most grateful for . . .

_____   _____

_____   _____

_____   _____

_____   _____

_____   _____

_____   _____

I couldn't say it at the time, but I felt . . .

_____   _____

_____   _____

_____   _____

_____   _____

_____   _____

_____   _____

_____   _____

_____   _____

Healing Our Fear

Relationships can be scary, especially new ones! You don't know how it's going to go, you're being vulnerable with someone new, you don't know the person very well yet, and anything could happen! All new love comes with some fear.

My biggest fears in the beginning were . . .

_____   _____

_____   _____

_____   _____

_____   _____

Strong relationships are a haven from fear. You helped me through mine by . . .

_____   _____

_____   _____

_____   _____

_____   _____

I feel fearless when you . . .

_____   _____

_____   _____

_____   _____

_____   _____

How I Knew

Nobody knows how they feel immediately. It takes some time to experience someone new, take the experience in, and search your soul to discover your true feelings. I didn't know right away, but when I knew, I knew.

I knew I wanted a committed relationship with you because . . .

_____   _____
_____   _____
_____   _____
_____   _____
_____   _____
_____   _____

I knew our relationship would last when . . .

_____   _____
_____   _____
_____   _____
_____   _____
_____   _____

You Make Me Better

Healthy relationships make us better. That's one of the reasons they're so important! There is almost no other way to experience such incredible growth than to share your life with someone.

Before I met you, I was . . .

_____   _____
_____   _____
_____   _____
_____   _____
_____   _____
_____   _____

Now that we're together, I am . . .

_____   _____
_____   _____
_____   _____
_____   _____
_____   _____

Our Epic Romance

Let's tell the story of how we met like it's the most romantic love story ever told. Let's make our story sound like the plot of an epic romance.

Using only true facts about how we met, let's elaborate and add color until we see the true beauty and magic in our story!

_____

_____

_____

_____

_____

_____

_____

_____

_____

_____

_____

HOW WE MET

Mementos

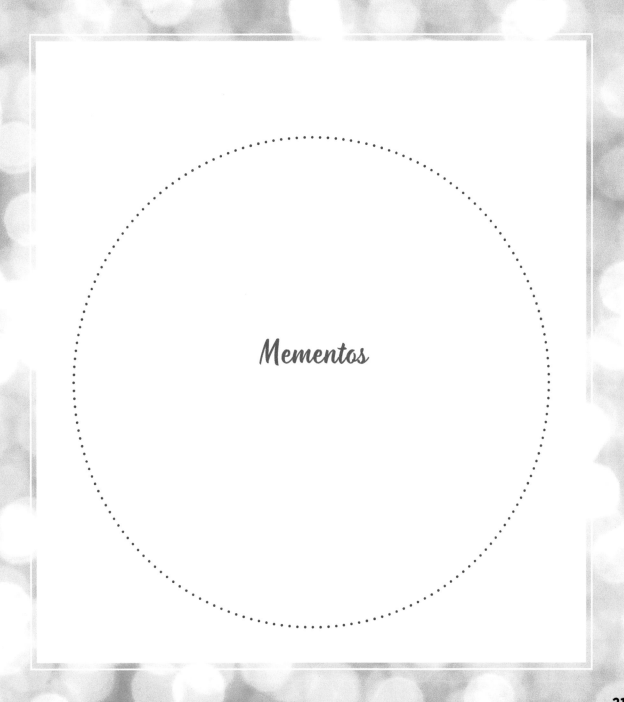

Mementos

PART 2

Adventures We've Taken

How blessed we are to have shared so much. To travel together, to learn and grow with each other, to overcome challenges with you by my side. We share our love in many ways, in many places, with many people. These adventures, big and small, are all part of our incredible journey. In this part, we'll reflect on the places we've explored, the memories we've made, and how our adventures impacted us.

Our Many Adventures

Adventures can be many things. Successes, failures, challenges, accomplishments, vacations, retreats, and even the mundane moments we share can become epic adventures in our minds when we reflect on them.

List the first three experiences that come to mind when you think of our adventures.

1. _____

_____

2. _____

_____

3. _____

_____

1. _____

_____

2. _____

_____

3. _____

_____

What does the word *adventure* mean to you?

_____   _____

_____   _____

_____   _____

_____   _____

_____   _____

Unpacking Our Adventures

For each of the three experiences listed in Our Many
Adventures (page 24), what made it an adventure?

_____   _____

_____   _____

_____   _____

_____   _____

_____   _____

Why were the experiences significant to me?

_____   _____

_____   _____

_____   _____

_____   _____

How did I grow because of them?

_____   _____

_____   _____

_____   _____

_____   _____

Our Top Five Adventures

We have truly shared some amazing experiences together,
so let's start with the best!

As a couple, let's pick our top five shared experiences that we unanimously agree on.

1. _____

2. _____

3. _____

4. _____

5. _____

What are your favorite memories from each experience? Think of one memory from each event and share why that moment was so special for you.

Our Travels

Travel enriches our lives. Whether it's to the next town,
across the country, or across the globe, it gets us out of our comfort zone,
exposes us to new things, and creates lifelong memories for us to share.

Let's note every trip we've taken together from the oldest
to the most recent and share our favorite moments from each.

_____

_____

_____

_____

When I think of our travels, I am most grateful for . . .

_____   _____

_____   _____

Of all the places we've visited, my favorite was . . .

_____   _____

_____   _____

A memory from one of our travels that will always be with me is . . .

_____   _____

_____   _____

New People and Places

As we see new places and meet new people, our own lives expand. As we deepen our understanding of life and others, we grow more within ourselves and our relationship.

Something that touched me in our travels
and changed the way I think about things is . . .

_____   _____
_____   _____
_____   _____
_____   _____
_____   _____
_____   _____

I think that experience stands out to me because . . .

_____   _____
_____   _____
_____   _____
_____   _____
_____   _____
_____   _____

The Extraordinary Everyday

As much as we love our travels, our adventures are so much more than
what we experience while we're on vacation or on a trip. Each day,
we experience adventures with each other: laughter, tears, frustrations,
fears, moments of peace and comfort, moments with children and/or pets,
times with friends and family, and time alone with each other.

Some of our daily adventures I look forward to the most are . . .

For our future daily adventures, I'd love to do more . . .

How You've Touched Me

A time you made me laugh until I cried was . . .

_____   _____
_____   _____
_____   _____

A time you touched my heart so deeply was . . .

_____   _____
_____   _____
_____   _____

A time that you surprised me was . . .

_____   _____
_____   _____

A time you comforted me when I really needed it was . . .

_____   _____
_____   _____

A time you showed up for me when I thought nobody would was . . .

_____   _____
_____   _____
_____   _____

Our Sexy Adventures

Some adventures don't even require us to leave the house, or the bedroom.

What are some of the sexy adventures we cherish?

_____   _____

_____   _____

_____   _____

What moments do we still think about to this day?

_____   _____

_____   _____

_____   _____

Are there things we might like to try again?

_____   _____

_____   _____

_____   _____

Anything we haven't tried yet and want to?

_____   _____

_____   _____

_____   _____

Our Wild Adventures

Our adventures aren't just about us! Sometimes we're pulled into adventures by the people we love when parents have an emergency, friends almost break up, or siblings need our help. Sometimes it seems like life itself is the adventure and we're just trying to keep up!

Let's reflect on the five most memorable events that have happened and had nothing to do with us.

_____   _____

_____   _____

_____   _____

_____   _____

_____   _____

How did we work together to support those we love?

_____   _____

_____   _____

_____   _____

_____   _____

_____   _____

Our Greatest Challenges

Amazing relationships are more than just a collection of good times together. Our love is special, not because it's always been easy but because we've stayed strong with each other through it all. Even when things are scary, our love is strong.

What are some of the biggest challenges we've overcome together?

_____   _____

_____   _____

_____   _____

_____   _____

_____   _____

How have these challenges strengthened our relationship?

_____   _____

_____   _____

_____   _____

_____   _____

_____   _____

How You've Been There

Our challenges create trust. Of course there have been times when our love felt uncertain, but during those times, our love overcame whatever challenge we were facing. Because of that, I trust you today.

Over time, you've shown up for me and earned my trust by . . .

_____   _____

_____   _____

_____   _____

_____   _____

_____   _____

_____   _____

I'll never forget the time you . . .

_____   _____

_____   _____

_____   _____

_____   _____

_____   _____

_____   _____

I Remember When . . .

I trust you because you've stayed by my side through
the difficult times, and that means so much to me.

One moment that reminds me of your strength and courage is . . .

Our Greatest Accomplishments

We can accomplish a lot on our own, but having you
by my side has allowed me to reach greater heights.

The biggest personal accomplishments I've made since we've been together are . . .

_____   _____

_____   _____

_____   _____

_____   _____

You have supported me in those accomplishments by . . .

_____   _____

_____   _____

_____   _____

_____   _____

When I was doing _____,   When I was doing _____,

you helped me by _____   you helped me by _____

_____,   _____,

and I couldn't have done it without you.   and I couldn't have done it without you.

I'm So Proud of You

One of the things that makes achieving anything amazing is knowing you are cheering me on and ready to celebrate every win together. Seeing your pride in me is the best feeling, and it makes every achievement a million times sweeter than it would have been alone.

I remember feeling your pride in me when . . .

Your pride in my accomplishments makes me feel like . . .

The Best Moments

Life can be very challenging and full of obstacles.
Because we have each other to share it all with, it feels easier.
We do it all to build a life together. Life is better when shared.

Some of my favorite moments to share with you are . . .

Our Next Adventure

What an adventure this life is! What an adventure our love is!
It's exciting to reflect on all we've been through, and it's exciting
to imagine what's yet to come for us. You are the person
I want to take all my adventures with, so let's plan our next one!

WHERE are we going?

_____

_____

_____

_____

WHEN will we go?

_____

_____

_____

_____

WHAT are we doing there?

_____

_____

_____

_____

_____

_____

HOW will we plan?

_____

_____

_____

_____

_____

_____

ADVENTURES WE'VE TAKEN

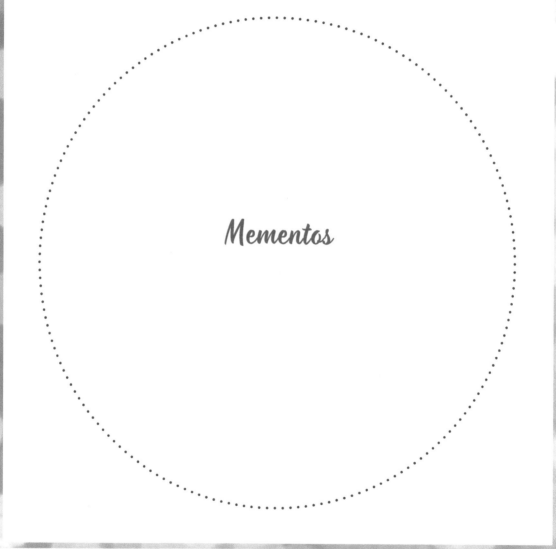

Mementos

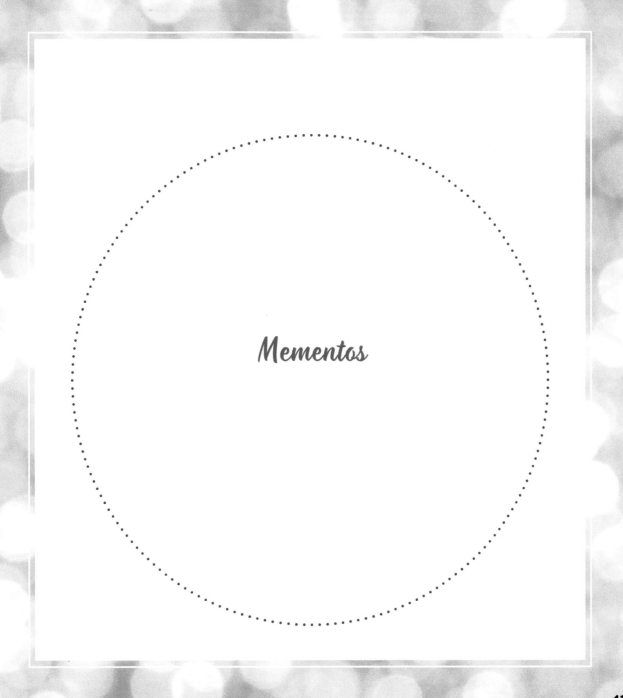

Mementos

PART 3

Our Loving Community

It has been said that it takes a village, and we know how blessed we are to have ours. One of the best things about our love is that we get to share it with the people we love the most. So many people have touched our lives and our hearts. Some made us who we are, and others helped along the way. Let's remember those who have been on this journey with us and reflect on how they've helped make our relationship what it is.

Our Family Tree

Some people are very close to their given family, whereas others are more connected to their chosen family, and some have amazing connections with both. Whether it's the family we're born with or the one we've chosen along the way, we are blessed to have them in our lives.

Let's fill in this family tree with the family members, given and chosen, that mean the most to us.

Our Favorite People

As we look at this tree, some names stand out more than others.
Certain people are extra special to us! They played a special
role in our relationship or inspired a special moment for us.

Let's each choose three people and write a few words about
who each person is and what makes them so special.

_____

is special to me because

_____

_____

is special to me because

_____

_____

is special to me because

_____

_____

_____

is special to me because

_____

_____

_____

is special to me because

_____

_____

_____

is special to me because

_____

_____

Our Caretakers

The people who raise us shape so much of our lives. In many ways, we become who we are because of them. Sometimes we try to emulate them, and other times we try to be their opposite. Either way, they are our first teachers. Let's take a moment to reflect on the lessons we learned from our parents and caregivers, and how that has shaped who we are and what we bring to our relationship.

Three lessons I learned from the people who raised me are . . .

1. _____

_____

_____

_____

2. _____

_____

_____

_____

3. _____

_____

_____

1. _____

_____

_____

_____

2. _____

_____

_____

_____

3. _____

_____

_____

Our Mother Figures

We all need to be nurtured in life. Perhaps we received this nourishment from the person who gave birth to us, or maybe it was from someone else who loved us. Whoever that person is, let's appreciate the mother figures in our lives, who they are, and the difference they've made for us.

The greatest mother figure in my life is

_____ ,

and I'm grateful to them because . . .

_____

_____

_____

_____

_____

_____

_____

The greatest mother figure in my life is

_____ ,

and I'm grateful to them because . . .

_____

_____

_____

_____

_____

_____

_____

Our Father Figures

We all need that dad energy in our life, whether it's provided by
our father or someone else who filled that role along the way.

Let's appreciate the father figures in our lives and how they have supported us.

The greatest father figure in my life is

_____,

and I'm grateful to them because . . .

_____

_____

_____

_____

_____

_____

_____

_____

_____

_____

The greatest father figure in my life is

_____,

and I'm grateful to them because . . .

_____

_____

_____

_____

_____

_____

_____

_____

_____

_____

Our Siblings

In truth, we are all siblings. Some of us grew up with siblings, and some of us adopted our own over time. Regardless of where they came from and how they came into our lives, the journey is so much richer because they are a part of it!

Who are the ones we consider family, whether by blood or not?

My siblings are _____   My siblings are _____

_____   _____

_____   _____

_____   _____

These people are so important to me because . . .

_____   _____

_____   _____

One of my favorite memories with these people is . . .

_____   _____

_____   _____

A memory I would love to make with these people is . . .

_____   _____

_____   _____

The Plans We Make

The plans we make with each other are exciting! And the plans we make together with those we love are a whole other level of exciting!

I hope, at some point, we get to take

_____

_____

with us and go _____

_____

_____

I hope, at some point, we get to take

_____

_____

with us and go _____

_____

_____

The Trip of a Lifetime

If we could choose six people to take the trip of a lifetime with, who would they be, where would we go, and what would we do?

Let's take . . .

1. _____

2. _____

3. _____

4. _____

5. _____

6. _____

We will go to . . .

_____

_____

_____

We will do . . .

_____

_____

_____

The Shoulders We Stand On

Life isn't always easy, and that's what our community is here for: to lift us up when we're down, to remind us we can overcome any challenge we face, and to listen when we need a supportive ear. Let's bring to mind and appreciate those who have been with us even when we weren't at our best.

Who are the friends who believed in us, even when we couldn't believe in ourselves?

_____   _____

_____   _____

The people who have shown up for me   The people who have shown up for me
when I really needed it are _____   when I really needed it are _____

_____   _____

_____   _____

When I felt alone and lost, I always knew   When I felt alone and lost, I always knew
I could call _____   I could call _____

_____   _____

_____   _____

When I was going through _____   When I was going through _____

_____   _____,

_____ was there   _____ was there

for me, and I'll never forget that.   for me, and I'll never forget that.

Who Played a Part?

In many ways, our community shapes our relationship. They often play a part in getting us together in the first place. They are the confidants and supportive friends we turn to over the years. But most of all, they are who we celebrate and share our joy with.

Feel free to answer the following as many times as you'd like to!

We might not be together if _____

_____

hadn't done _____

_____.

_____ has been there for us more times than we can count.

_____

is always ready to celebrate our wins, and we love him/her/them for it!

We might not be together if _____

_____

hadn't done _____.

_____.

_____ has been there for us more times than we can count.

_____

is always ready to celebrate our wins, and we love him/her/them for it!

Who We Turn To

Relationships aren't always easy, and we, like all couples, know that we have had our challenges. Our community reminds us how special our love really is. They remember who we are even when we temporarily forget.

In our relationship, when we've had challenges, I'm grateful that _____ _____was always cheering us on to overcome them.

During some of our challenges, I spoke to

_____

about it, and they gave me some amazing advice.

In our relationship, when we've had challenges, I'm grateful that _____ _____ was always cheering us on to overcome them.

During some of our challenges, I spoke to

_____

about it, and they gave me some amazing advice.

Our Communities

When we get involved in things together, we grow. Being part of a larger community allows us to see and experience parts of ourselves and each other that we would otherwise miss out on. That could be a religious community, a service organization, a fitness group, a personal development program, or anything else that speaks to us.

What are the communities we love, and how have they supported us over the years?

Where We Grow

What are the environments where we've grown the most? It could
be a childhood home, our first apartment, our place
of employment, or any other place where growth has occurred.

Describe them and why they are significant in our lives.

_____   _____
_____   _____
_____   _____
_____   _____
_____   _____
_____   _____
_____   _____
_____   _____
_____   _____
_____   _____
_____   _____

Who We Grow With

Who are the people we've experienced the most growth around? Are they coworkers, college friends, or friends from a local community service group?

Describe them and our relationship with them.

Who We've Lost

People move in and out of our lives. Some come for a day and some for a season, and some will remain on the journey with us for life.

Who are those special people we've lost touch with and who we still think about?
If you could send them a message, what would it be?

The Community to Come

Community enriches our lives, breaks up the mundane, inspires us to be better people, and brings so much joy!

As we imagine our community in the future, how might we like it to grow and expand in the years to come?

_____   _____

_____   _____

_____   _____

_____   _____

What new things might we want to get involved in?

_____   _____

_____   _____

_____   _____

_____   _____

What new hobbies and activities might we take on, either together or separately?

_____   _____

_____   _____

_____   _____

_____   _____

OUR LOVING COMMUNITY

Mementos

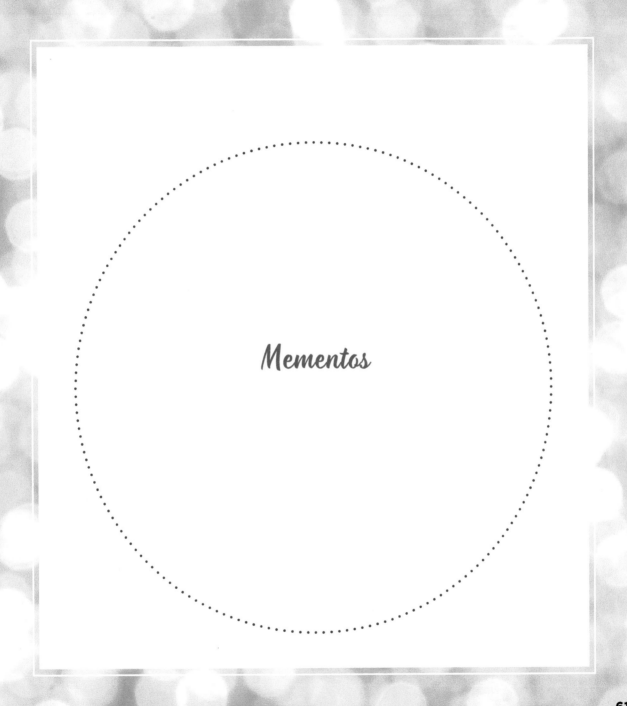

Mementos

PART 4

Celebrating Special Occasions

The special moments of our lives commemorate our journey together. We celebrate the days we were born, the accomplishments we achieve, the holidays we love, and the passing years. We find special moments each week to remember our love as we reflect on this journey together. These significant moments stand out like highlights in our mind, reminding us of all the magic we've shared and the magic that's yet to come.

Celebrating with You

When I think of celebrating with you, the first image that comes to mind is . . .

We were doing _____   We were doing _____
                  (activity)   *(activity)*

_____   _____

in _____   in _____
              (location)   *(location)*

_____,   _____,

and we were wearing _____.   and we were wearing _____.
                       (clothing)   *(clothing)*

We were celebrating . . .

_____   _____

_____   _____

When I saw you that day, I felt . . .

_____   _____

_____   _____

That moment is so special to me because . . .

_____   _____

_____   _____

Our Celebrations

Let's celebrate our life and love.

We've been together for _____ ☐ Months | ☐ Years
and in that time we've celebrated:

List each significant celebration that comes to mind for both of you.

_____

_____

_____

My favorite of these is _____

_____ because

_____ .

The celebration that is most sentimental

to me is _____

because _____

_____ .

The most fun we've ever had celebrating

was _____ ,

and that is, of course, because of _____

_____ .

My favorite of these is _____

_____ because

_____ .

The celebration that is most sentimental

to me is _____

because _____

_____ .

The most fun we've ever had celebrating

was _____ ,

and that is, of course, because of _____

_____ .

The Holiday Season

The holiday season is such a special time of year. No matter what we are celebrating, the atmosphere is full of cheer and good vibes all around. It's such a special time to be with each other and to be in love!

Our first holiday season together was in _____, and we celebrated by . . .
(year)

_____

_____

That year, I remember _____

_____

about you, and that memory stands out

to me because _____

_____

That year, I remember _____

_____

about you, and that memory stands out

to me because _____

_____

We've now spent _____ holiday seasons together.
(number of)

My favorite holiday with you was

_____

because _____

_____.

My favorite holiday with you was

_____

because _____

_____.

Giving of Gifts

Gifts are such a special way to show our love. They show how
well we know each other and how much we keep the other on our minds.

The best gift you ever gave me was . . .

Our Birthdays

On our birthdays each year, we celebrate each other! We take a day to appreciate the birth and life of the one we love and how grateful we are for their existence. Let's fill in our partner's birthday and, just for fun, their astrological sign, too!

My partner's birthday is _____ and they are a _____.
(sign)

My favorite birthday I've shared with you was _____ because _____.

Once, for my birthday, you did _____,

and that meant so much to me because _____

My birthday could have been awful that year, but it wasn't because you _____.

My partner's birthday is _____ and they are a _____.
(sign)

My favorite birthday I've shared with you was _____ because _____.

Once, for my birthday, you did _____,

and that meant so much to me because _____

My birthday could have been awful that year, but it wasn't because you _____.

Our Anniversary

Each year, we can celebrate our love, renew our commitment,
and remember how special this love of ours really is.

Our anniversary is _____, and on that day, we

commemorate our _____

(wedding/first date, etc.)

For anniversaries, I prefer to . . .

☐ Travel ☐ Stay home ☐ Travel ☐ Stay home

☐ Dine out ☐ Cook at home ☐ Dine out ☐ Cook at home

☐ Get dressed up ☐ Be casual ☐ Get dressed up ☐ Be casual

I enjoy our anniversaries most when we . . .

_____ _____

_____ _____

_____ _____

The dream anniversary celebration of a lifetime for me is . . .

_____ _____

_____ _____

_____ _____

Our Growth

Growth is the mark of an amazing partnership. Our love inspires us to be better in all areas of life; we accomplish more because of the love we share. It helps us feel safe, secure, confident, and worthy.

What are some of the major accomplishments
we've each made since we've been together?

I Acknowledge Myself for . . .

Your achievements are our achievements.

One thing I am particularly proud of myself for is . . .

_____   _____
_____   _____

One thing I am particularly proud of you for is . . .

_____   _____
_____   _____

You've helped me achieve my goals in life by . . .

_____   _____
_____   _____

Something we've achieved together because we worked together is . . .

_____
_____
_____

As a couple, we are most proud of ourselves for . . .

_____
_____

The Children We Nurture

Children bring such magic to our lives; they remind us of the innocence within each of us. They dare us to dream and push the boundaries of our creativity. They remind us of how simple love and relationships can be when we don't complicate them. Maybe we've been influenced by the children we raised; maybe we have the honor of being an aunt, an uncle, or a big cousin; or perhaps we have simply been blessed to experience the children of our friends and others around us.

Who are the children we've nurtured, and how have we celebrated that?

The Pets We Adore

Pets bring out the child in us! They remind us that it's okay to play, to not take life too seriously, and they love us, even on our worst days.

Whether they are part of our family or belong to those close to us, who are the pets we love?

The Best, the Worst, and Everything in Between

Our journey has not been linear. It has included some of the best experiences, the worst moments, and everything in between.
We can't forget to celebrate ourselves for being here today having overcome these challenges and lived to tell the story about it.

What are some of the major challenges that we've overcome together, and what have we learned from them?

_____

_____

_____

_____

_____

_____

_____

_____

_____

_____

_____

_____

The Greatest Challenge of Our Lives

Challenges only make us stronger.

I think the biggest challenge of our lives was . . .

_____   _____

_____   _____

I overcame that challenge by . . .

_____   _____

_____   _____

_____   _____

Something amazing I saw in you at that time was . . .

_____   _____

_____   _____

_____   _____

The way you supported me through that was . . .

_____   _____

_____   _____

_____   _____

Celebrating Life

Celebrating is about more than just holidays and birthdays.
We celebrate life because each moment is special and an opportunity
to share and experience our love with each other.

From spontaneous romantic evenings to thoughtful surprises
to moments when we fall asleep in each other's arms, what are some
everyday things in our life together that are worth celebrating?

Being Spontaneous

Sometimes you don't need an elaborate plan or a plan at all.

I'll never forget the best spontaneous date we ever had when . . .

My favorite part was when . . .

The Most Special Thing

> **When the most thoughtful gesture comes out of seemingly nowhere, it makes me fall for you all over again.**

The most special thing you did for me, for no reason at all, was . . .

I especially loved how you . . .

Celebrations to Come

As we look to our future together, we know there will be many wonderful things to celebrate. As the years go by, we become wiser, more confident, and less hard on ourselves, and we allow ourselves to celebrate more.

Let's consider the celebrations that lie ahead. What is it that we're looking forward to, and how might we want to celebrate these special events?

CELEBRATING
SPECIAL OCCASIONS

Mementos

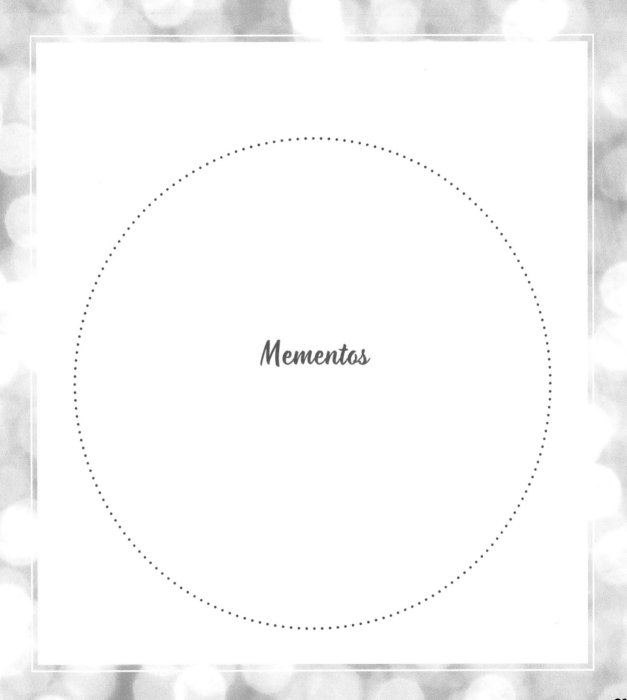

Mementos

PART 5

Our Love Today

The best thing about our life is that we share it with each other. We are blessed to wake up and go to sleep together, to take walks and go for drives together, to cook and eat together. We get to laugh till our sides hurt and fall asleep in each other's arms. We support each other in the tough times and celebrate the good times. We are not on this journey alone. We are traveling it with a loving partner who cares deeply, and there is nobody else I'd rather be on this journey with.

How We Wake Up

As the sun peeks through our blinds and we begin to awaken, what are the first things we do? Do we roll into each other's arms, take some time by ourselves to prepare for the day, or rush to the kitchen to get the coffee going?

Let's take a moment to reflect on how our days begin
and how that supports us as we launch into the day.

Each Morning You . . .

Every morning is a start of a new journey with you.

Something you do each morning that supports me is . . .

_____ _____
_____ _____
_____ _____

Something I look forward to each morning with you is . . .

_____ _____
_____ _____
_____ _____

I am happy to wake up with you because . . .

_____ _____
_____ _____
_____ _____

What I love most about our mornings is . . .

_____ _____
_____ _____
_____ _____

Making Every Morning Great

Let's face it—not all mornings get off to a great start. Sometimes there's just not enough time. We're behind, overwhelmed, stressed out, and tired. We spend much of our lives trudging through a difficult morning alone, but now we have each other. We are not alone. We are a team, and we can work together to get every day off to the right start.

Let's strategize! How can we set up each morning, as a team, to make sure we both get a great start to our day?

Checking In

Each day, we deal with a million little things—work, pets, kids,
taking care of our physical and mental health, eating well, sleeping well,
and still making time to enjoy ourselves a little each day. It can be
a lot—so much, in fact, that we might not always be aware of what's going
on with each other. Let's take a moment to check in.

Something that's been on my mind a lot lately is . . .

_____   _____

_____   _____

Something I've been feeling good about is . . .

_____   _____

_____   _____

Something I've been feeling not so good about is . . .

_____   _____

_____   _____

Something I've wanted to ask you for but haven't yet is . . .

_____   _____

_____   _____

The Day's Treasures

Every day has a treasure in it. Even if the day was tough,
there is something to look forward to, something to be excited about.

The treasures in my days are . . .

I Count on You to . . .

You are always there when I need someone to lean on.

Every day, I smile because I can count on you to . . .

_____   _____
_____   _____
_____   _____
_____   _____
_____   _____
_____   _____

Every day, I smile because I can count on you to . . .

_____   _____
_____   _____
_____   _____
_____   _____
_____   _____
_____   _____

The Best Time of Day

Every minute, every hour with you is precious.

My favorite part of each day is

_____
(time)

when we _____,
(activity)

and I love it so much because . . .

_____

_____

_____

_____

_____

_____

My favorite part of each day is

_____
(time)

when we _____,
(activity)

and I love it so much because . . .

_____

_____

_____

_____

_____

_____

Our Responsibilities

It's been said that the quality of our lives is equal to the responsibility that we have, and we have lot of it! From the parts of us we put out in the world each day to the parts of us we share only at home, our plates are full.

What are some of the things that we're responsible for (together and individually)?

_____   _____

_____   _____

_____   _____

_____   _____

How do these things enrich our lives and make us better people?

_____   _____

_____   _____

_____   _____

_____   _____

_____   _____

_____   _____

_____   _____

Our Play

Responsibility is a big piece of the puzzle, but it's not the whole puzzle. We all need to release the pressure on a regular basis to prevent an explosion! We work hard, we play hard, and that's what makes our life amazing! Let's take a look at how we play.

Some of my favorite times with you are when we . . .

_____   _____

_____   _____

We can have a perfect date night just by . . .

_____   _____

_____   _____

It is so much fun to just _____   It is so much fun to just _____

_____   _____

with you.   with you.

Activities we love to share together are . . .

_____   _____

_____   _____

When we can, we are definitely going to . . .

_____   _____

_____   _____

Each Day, We . . .

Every day I leave with the thought of returning to you.

Every day, I _____
_____(go to work/care for children, etc.)_

_____

and you _____
_____(go to work/care for children, etc.)_

_____.

Every day, I _____
_____(go to work/care for children, etc.)_

_____

and you _____
_____(go to work/care for children, etc.)_

_____.

I appreciate what you do because . . .

_____

_____

_____

_____

I admire you for . . .

_____

_____

_____

_____

Thank you for . . .

_____

_____

_____

_____

Eating Together

The dinner table is the heart of every home. On busy nights, we pick up takeout, and when we have time, we cook a meal with love that we can enjoy together.

Some of our favorite things to cook and eat together are . . .

Just for Fun!

It's important each day to include something that's just for fun, whether that's an hour of our favorite show, relaxing with a glass of wine and a good book, or taking a bubble bath (alone or together). Winding down together is how we complete the day and prepare our hearts and minds for the day to come.

Our favorite ways to wind down are . . .

_____   _____

_____   _____

_____   _____

Some of our favorite shows to binge-watch are . . .

_____   _____

_____   _____

Some of our favorite books and movies are . . .

_____   _____

_____   _____

Some other exciting evening activities are . . .

_____   _____

_____   _____

_____   _____

Breaking the Routine

Our routines support us, but they aren't everything. We love the feeling of release when we drop the routine for a day, a week, or even a few weeks, and allow ourselves to explore life outside of the mundane.

Some of our favorite ways to spend our free time are . . .

_____   _____

_____   _____

_____   _____

On the weekends, we like to . . .

_____   _____

_____   _____

Some things we like to enjoy together are . . .

_____   _____

_____   _____

_____   _____

Some things we like to enjoy separately are . . .

_____   _____

_____   _____

Our Recent Memories

We've made a lot of memories recently. Some are bigger than others, but over the last few months/years, there have been so many things that we will cherish in the years to come.

Let's make a note of them now and reflect on why these moments are special to us.

Those Who Surround Us

The people in our lives today may not be the same people who have been there in the past. They are unique for this chapter. In the same way that many of the people from the last chapter may not have made it to this one, some of those we are close to now will go their own way as time goes on.

Who are we closest to in our life right now, what gifts do these people bring to our lives, and why they are perfect for this chapter of our lives?

Our Dreams

We never stop dreaming. We have a vision for our life that is growing and evolving as we do. What is it that we are dreaming about right now?

What are the things we're wishing for and calling into our life?

OUR LOVE TODAY

Mementos

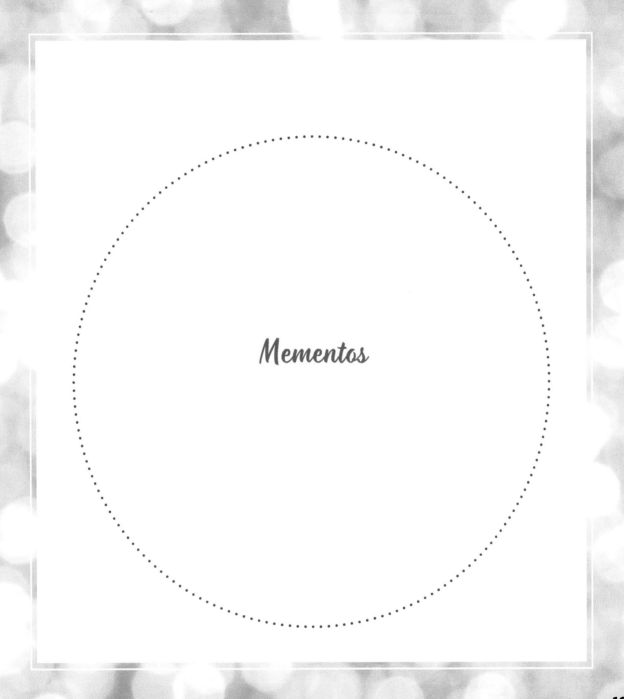

Mementos

PART 6

Picturing Our Future Together

The most exciting part of our lives isn't what's happened already but what's still to come. I can't wait to watch our dreams become a reality. Whether it's building a dream home and nest egg, raising a family, or going on globe-trotting adventures, the best part is knowing that you'll be by my side through it all. Whenever we fall, we'll be there to catch each other. Let's dream together.

What I See in Our Future

When I think of our future together, some of the images that come to mind are . . .

_____   _____

_____   _____

I see us in an urban/rural environment.   I see us in an urban/rural environment.

_____   _____

_____   _____

I feel warm weather/cool weather on   I feel warm weather/cool weather on
my skin.   my skin.

_____   _____

_____   _____

I think of us spending our time doing . . .   I think of us spending our time doing . . .

_____   _____

_____   _____

Getting on the Same Page

Did we answer the questions from "What I See in Our Future" (page 104) the same or differently? Let's explore that together. Where they are the same, let's clarify and make commitments about it! Where it's different, let's compromise and be creative!

How can everybody win here?

_____

_____

_____

_____

_____

_____

_____

_____

_____

_____

_____

_____

_____

Asking for More

Most people don't ask too much from life; they ask too little. As human beings, we suffer from chronic reasonableness and, therefore, don't dream as outrageously as we could. The funny thing is that even if we accomplish only half of our outrageous dreams, we usually still go further than we would without them.

Let's be outrageous together! If there were no limitations
on what we could be, do, or have, what would our future look like?

_____

_____

_____

_____

_____

_____

_____

_____

_____

_____

_____

_____

_____

Vision Boarding

Clarity is key; you must be able to see the vision in front of you.
Let's bring the vision to life! Draw it out, or use magazine
clippings, pictures, sentimental items, or anything that speaks to you.

Try to capture not only what it looks like but also what it feels like.

Let's Get Real

Now let's get real and share what's really on our hearts when it comes to the future. Let's hear each other, support each other, and encourage each other so we can come out of this envisioning more possibility in our future . . .

My most heartfelt hopes for my life are . . .

_____   _____
_____   _____

Something I've always wanted but I'm afraid I'll never have is . . .

_____   _____
_____   _____

Something I'd like to do but I don't think I can is . . .

_____   _____
_____   _____

A childhood dream that I let go of a long time ago is . . .

_____   _____
_____   _____

If I had no limitations of any kind, I would . . .

_____   _____
_____   _____

The Circle of Life

What tangible goals do we want to work on together? The circle-of-life chart can help us assess where we are right now and lead us in some inspiring new directions around the things that matter most to us. Let's each fill in the chart in a different color so we can see our answers clearly.

In each domain of the chart, assess where you currently feel like you are in that area of your life: 10 being amazing and 1 being awful.
Use a different color from your partner, and put a number in each domain.

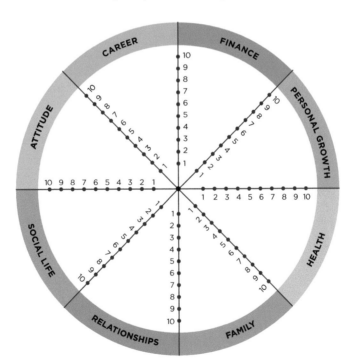

Areas of Improvement

For each of us, what are the three domains where we desire the most improvement? Let's share with each other what we feel is missing in each of those areas and how we feel it could be improved.

In other words, what would we like to see in each of these areas?

It's important here to listen with an open heart and have this conversation in the spirit of dreaming together rather than having a conversation about what's wrong.

1. _____

2. _____

3. _____

_____

_____

_____

_____

_____

1. _____

2. _____

3. _____

_____

_____

_____

_____

_____

_____

_____

_____

Goals to Aspire to

Based on our answers in the circle-of-life exercise (page 109),
what are some goals we may want to begin working
toward both in our personal lives and together as a couple?

_____   _____

_____   _____

_____   _____

_____   _____

_____   _____

_____

_____

_____

_____

_____

_____

_____

_____

Commitments to Make

Today:

_____   _____

_____   _____

This week:

_____   _____

_____   _____

This month:

_____   _____

_____   _____

_____

_____

_____

_____

Envisioning the Future

Where would we like to be financially?

_____   _____

_____   _____

How do we see our health and fitness evolving?

_____   _____

_____   _____

What changes do we want to see to our mindset and spirituality?

_____   _____

_____   _____

How do we envision our friendships and extended family relationships?

_____   _____

_____   _____

In what state do we picture our family?

_____   _____

How might we like our careers to grow and expand in the years to come?

_____   _____

_____   _____

Our Bucket Lists!

What are the items on our bucket lists, and do we even have a bucket list? If not, let's create one! Consider all the things one can experience in life and try to consider this without unnecessary limitations. You can figure out how it's all going to happen later.

For now, just think of anything and everything that you'd like to experience in this life and get it out on paper!

This Year . . .

_____   _____

_____   _____

_____   _____

_____   _____

_____   _____

_____   _____

_____   _____

_____   _____

_____   _____

_____   _____

_____   _____

_____   _____

Who We Want to See More

Who do we want to be around the most as the years go by? Are there distant family and friends we want to see more often? Do we want to spend more time with our children? Do we want to make more quality time to be together?

Let's consider, as we build these dreams, who we want to share them with the most.

Where We Want to Go

What are the adventures we want to take and places we'd like to travel to?

How We Want to Feel

How do we want to feel each day about ourselves, our life, our habits and practices? If you could pick three or four words that describe how we want to wake up and live each day of our lives, what would those words be?

How Our Love Will Grow

How do we see our love growing in the years to come? What do we want to feel for and with each other later in life? As we complete this book together, let's clarify the vision we have for the love that we are growing each day.

_____

_____

_____

_____

_____

_____

_____

_____

_____

_____

_____

_____

_____

_____

_____

_____

_____

_____

PICTURING OUR FUTURE TOGETHER

Mementos

About the Author

Shane Kohler has worked in personal development and transformation for over a decade. He has led seminars throughout the United States, personally coached more than 100 people, helped dozens of couples bring their relationships back from the brink of collapse, and created a framework for singles to consciously create lifelong, committed partnerships with their ideal partners. He cofounded the Living Relationship with his beautiful wife, Fatima, and their passion revolves around helping people create the love that most will only ever dream about. Shane currently lives with his wife, Fatima, and puppy, Ollie, just outside of New York City and spends his free time chasing the most beautiful views he can find on planet Earth.

Learn more at thelivingrelationship.com and follow him on Instagram at @the_living_relationship.

MY LETTER TO YOU:

Looking Forward to the Memories to Come

MY LETTER TO YOU:

Looking Forward to the Memories to Come

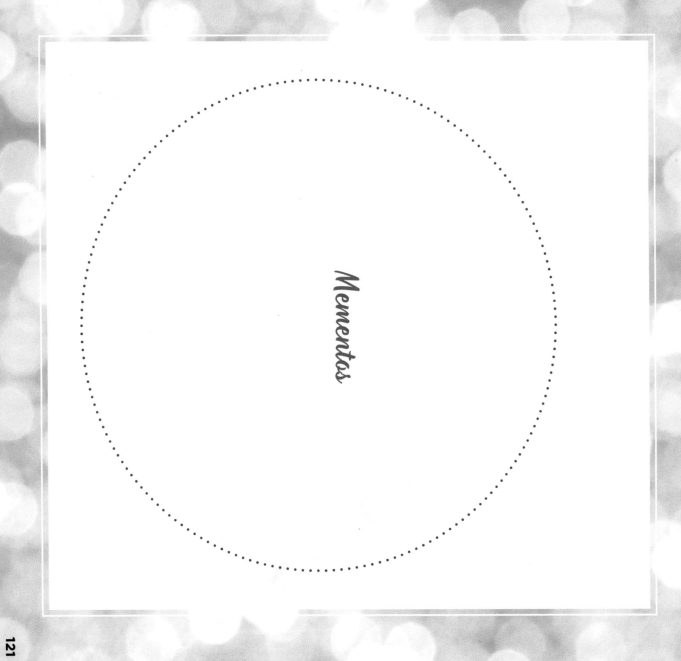

Mementos